THE KING'S PICTURES

VAN DYCK

Windsor

CHARLES I (96)

145 × 106 in.

THE KING'S PICTURES

AN ILLUSTRATED SOUVENIR OF
THE EXHIBITION OF THE KING'S
PICTURES AT THE ROYAL
ACADEMY OF ARTS, LONDON
1946-47

ROYAL ACADEMY OF ARTS

GENERAL INFORMATION

The Exhibition opens on Saturday, October 26, 1946, and closes on Sunday, March 16, 1947.

Hours of Admission:
      Week-days, 10 A.M. to 7 P.M.
      Sundays, 2 to 7 P.M.

Price of Admission: 1s. 6d.

Price of Catalogue: 1s. 6d.

Price of Illustrated Souvenir: 5s.

Season Tickets: £1 5s.

Reduced Price Tickets.

Principals of recognised Schools of Art can obtain Season Tickets for Art Students on their registers at the special rate of 7s. 6d.

Principals of all Schools can obtain single tickets at half-price (9d.) in lots of 10 or more, for the use of their pupils.

Secretaries of Staff Associations, Working Men's or Girls' Clubs, or similar organisations, can obtain single tickets at 1s. in lots of 10 or more, for the use of their members.

Visitors are required to give up their sticks and umbrellas before entering the Galleries; they must be left with the attendants at the Cloak Room in the Entrance Hall. The other attendants are strictly forbidden to take charge of anything.

Invalids may obtain the use of a wheeled chair during certain hours, without charge, by previous arrangement with the Secretary, to whom application should be made for the necessary order.

Post-cards of a selection of the Exhibits are on sale in the Vestibule, and orders can there be given for photographs of the pictures.

THE ROYAL ACADEMY SCHOOLS

The Schools of the Royal Academy date from its foundation in 1768, and are open to duly qualified students in Painting, Sculpture and Architecture. No fees are charged. The Architecture School remains closed for the present.

The cost of maintaining the Schools is defrayed entirely from the admission money paid by the public who visit the Exhibitions of the Royal Academy.

The Library of the Royal Academy is primarily intended for the use of Members and Students; but exhibitors and persons engaged in serious research are welcome to use it on application made to the Secretary.

Among the 6,000 Students who have passed through the Schools since the formation were Lawrence, Beechey, Hoppner, Soane, Flaxman, Turner, Wilkie, Constable, Etty, Landseer, Frith, Millais and Watts.

PREFACE

By the gracious act of its Patron, His Majesty The King, the Royal Academy is enabled to produce for 1946–47 a Winter Exhibition of unique importance and interest—a rare privilege and opportunity for which all art-lovers must feel profoundly grateful. This Exhibition of The King's Pictures contains more than five hundred paintings in the Royal Collection, selected from all the Palaces in which the Collection is permanently kept, and including a large number of works which are not normally accessible to the public.

The Exhibition has been planned to show, in one great range of our Galleries, the unrivalled series of portraits of notable figures in British history, in which the development of portraiture from the reign of King Henry VIII to that of Queen Victoria is illustrated by masterpieces of Holbein, Van Dyck, Reynolds, Gainsborough, Lawrence and others. After this, appear in succession the principal works in the collection of King Charles I, which were recovered at the Restoration after having been sold by the Commonwealth ; Venetian paintings acquired by our Founder, King George III; sporting pictures by Stubbs and Ben Marshall, mainly acquired by King George IV when Prince of Wales; many fine Dutch paintings bought for King George IV; early Italian works collected by the Prince Consort; and popular subject pictures by outstanding artists of the Victorian era. Not only has the Exhibition the glory of containing many masterpieces of the greatest painters of Europe, but also the interest of showing the several main stages in the growth of this historic Collection, which has been built up by the contributions of a succession of Sovereigns according to the tendencies of their personal tastes.

The Royal Academy is most sincerely grateful, in the first place, to His Majesty for the signal act of favour which has brought this splendid Exhibition into existence; and also to the Joint Committee of Members of the Royal Household and of the Royal Academy who have planned and organised it. The selection of the exhibits has been made by Sir Gerald F. Kelly, R.A., Messrs. Anthony Blunt (Surveyor of The King's Pictures), Ellis K. Waterhouse and Benedict Nicolson. The work of compiling the catalogue has been done, for the portraits and Dutch paintings, by Mr. Waterhouse; for the Italian works of the 14th–16th Centuries, by Mr. Nicolson; for the subject pictures of Rubens and Van Dyck, by Dr. L. Burchard; and for the remaining works, by Mr. Blunt, with assistance for the early Flemish and German works from Mr. Martin Davies of the National Gallery and Dr. F. Grossmann.

ALFRED J. MUNNINGS,
President.

EXHIBITION OF THE KING'S PICTURES

COMMITTEE

Sir ULICK ALEXANDER, K.C.V.O. (*Chairman*)

Sir Alfred J. Munnings, P.R.A.   Sir Terence E. G. Nugent, K.C.V.O.

Sir Gerald F. Kelly, R.A.   Sir Owen F. Morshead, K.C.V.O.

W. T. Monnington, R.A.   Anthony Blunt

HANGING COMMITTEE

Sir Alfred J. Munnings, P.R.A.   The Hon. Sir Richard F. Molyneux, K.C.V.O.

Sir Walter W. Russell, C.V.O., R.A.   Anthony Blunt

Sir Gerald F. Kelly, R.A.   Benedict Nicolson

A. R. Thomson, R.A.   E. K. Waterhouse

Secretary.   *Assistant Secretary.*

Sir WALTER R. M. LAMB, K.C.V.O.   BENEDICT NICOLSON.

LECTURES

THE HISTORY OF THE ROYAL COLLECTION

THE following Lectures, illustrated by lantern slides, will be given in the Reynolds Room of the Royal Academy at 5 p.m.

Date	Subject	Lecturer
Nov. 1, 1946	Charles I	Anthony Blunt
Nov. 8 ,,	Rubens and Van Dyck in England	Prof. Emile Cammaerts, C.B.E.
Nov. 15 ,,	George III: the Smith and Albani Collections	Anthony Blunt
Nov. 22 ,,	Royal Portraiture	Ellis K. Waterhouse
Nov. 29 ,,	George IV's Dutch Pictures	Prof. van Regteren Altena
Dec. 6 ,,	George IV and the Waterloo Chamber	The Hon. Harold Nicolson, C.M.G.
Dec. 13 ,,	Queen Victoria and the Prince Consort	Sir Owen Morshead, K.C.V.O.

Price of Tickets : For the Series, 15*s.*; for Single Lectures, 2*s.* 6*d.* each. Obtainable from The Secretary, Royal Academy of Arts, Piccadilly, W.1.

INTRODUCTION

LIKE all private collections, that formed by the Kings and Queens of England reflects the tastes of those who formed it. Naturally the Collection is richest in works of the English School, and among that School in examples of the portrait painters. It is an immemorial custom of sovereigns to employ artists to record in pictorial form themselves, their families and the members of their courts, and it would be difficult to bring together a group of portraits more representative of what this art achieved in England than those now collected in the Royal Academy. The formal and precise portraiture of the Tudors reached its highest expression in the art of its creator, Holbein, here represented by some of his most impressive and some of his most delicate works. His followers in England elaborated his manner, to suit the more esoteric mentality of the Elizabethan age, without however making any fundamental innovations. In the reign of James I a new generation of foreign artists, such as van Somer and Mytens, was imported to work for the Court, but it was not till the advent of Van Dyck in 1632 that English portraiture was set on new lines. Van Dyck succeeded in England because he found the precise formula needed to express that particular elegance which the cultured Charles I created at his Court, with the assistance of men like Lord Arundel, eminent alike for rank, learning, taste and political wisdom. As in the case of Holbein, so with Van Dyck, the original formula was elaborated but not improved by his successors, from Lely to Kneller, and the spark of life does not fully return to official English portraiture till the generation of Reynolds and Gainsborough. The patronage of George III leant towards the latter, whose intimate understanding of character suited the homely outlook of the King. Reynolds, on the other hand, was above all successful in official portraiture, and the finest examples of his art here displayed represent either members of the Royal Family who took an active part in public life or those who, like Lord Rodney or Lord Keppel, were the servants of the Crown in the armed forces. In Lawrence the succeeding generation found a master who combined something of the formal grandeur of Reynolds with Gainsborough's insight into character; and never did he have a finer opportunity of displaying these talents than in the series of portraits commissioned by George IV, when Prince Regent, to decorate the Waterloo Chamber which he had conceived to celebrate those who had contributed to the downfall of Napoleon. The solid formality of the Victorian Court could not perhaps produce an artist of this quality, but no one could reflect more precisely than Winterhalter its severe and impressive sincerity.

The Kings of England were not, however, solely concerned with the commissioning of portraits. Two among them at least, Charles I and George IV, must rank among the most enthusiastic collectors of earlier painting. It is to the part of the collection of Charles I recovered after the Commonwealth sale that we owe the masterpieces of Venetian painting in the present Exhibition, though these represent but a fraction of the treasures which he assembled. Nevertheless the two great compositions by Tintoretto, the portraits by Titian, Tintoretto and Leandro Bassano, and Giorgione's *Shepherd* could hold their own in any display of Venetian painting. Nor was the taste of Charles I confined to the art of Venice, for the other Italian schools are represented in no mean degree by the works of Correggio, Andrea del Sarto, Dosso Dossi, and many others.

In the 18th Century two further members of the Royal Family made important additions to the Collection. Frederick, Prince of Wales, the father of George III, acquired many fine works of Rubens and Van Dyck, as well as paintings by French and Italian masters of the 17th Century. His son, apart from encouraging the historical painting of Benjamin West, secured the entire collection of Venetian and other paintings formed by Joseph Smith, English consul in Venice, and so brought to England the unrivalled series of paintings by Canaletto of which the greater number are here shown.

George IV was a specialist in Dutch and Flemish art, and by a judicious series of purchases from the London sale rooms brought together a group of paintings of these schools which can bear comparison with any in the world. Not only are the great figures, such as Rembrandt, admirably represented, but certain artists of the second rank, particularly Cuyp and Teniers, can here be seen in examples which give an almost new idea of their talents.

The last great additions to the Royal Collection were made by the Prince Consort, whose imagination was fired by the art of the primitives at a time when they were almost wholly neglected. Like all explorers in a new field he was at times misled, and some of the works which he acquired are now considered of secondary importance ; but these are more than offset by the few precious Italian paintings of the 14th and 15th Centuries which his insight led him to buy, notably the Duccio and the Gentile da Fabriano.

The Royal Collection cannot, from its very nature, present a complete picture of European art through its various phases. But the great groups of paintings enumerated above provide a rare storehouse of certain aspects of its achievements, and reflect at the same time the individual tastes of those who through four centuries have contributed to its formation.   A. F. B.

Permission has been graciously given by His Majesty
The King to reproduce the works illustrated in this
volume, and the copyright is in every case strictly reserved.

GENTILE DA FABRIANO   THE MADONNA AND CHILD (176)
Buckingham Palace   55½ × 32½ in.

11

12

THE DEATH OF SIMON MAGUS (180)
$9\frac{1}{2} \times 14$ in.

BENOZZO GOZZOLI
Buckingham Palace

13

LORENZO COSTA   LADY WITH A LAP-DOG (177)
Windsor   17½ × 13 in.

GIOVANNI BELLINI   YOUNG MAN (159)
Hampton Court   17 × 13½ in.

14

141 NORTH ITALIAN SCHOOL A LADY IN A GREEN DRESS (218)

Hampton Court 29¼ × 24¼ in.

ANDREA DEL SARTO PORTRAIT OF A WOMAN (213)

Windsor 25½ × 19¾ in.

GIULIO ROMANO
Hampton Court

ISABELLA D'ESTE (231)
$44\frac{1}{2} \times 35$ in.

PARMIGIANINO   PORTRAIT OF A BOY (227)
Windsor   38 × 32 in.

17

CORREGGIO   HOLY FAMILY (246)

Hampton Court   27 × 22 in.

ST. CATHERINE (244)

24 × 20 in.

CORREGGIO

Hampton Court

18

ANDREA ODONI (217)

40 × 45¾ in.

LORENZO LOTTO

Hampton Court

ANDREA DEL SARTO
Windsor

THE VIRGIN AND CHILD WITH ST. JOHN (214)
$39\frac{1}{2} \times 29\frac{1}{2}$ in.

TITIAN   LANDSCAPE (211)
Buckingham Palace   46 × 38¾ in.

21

JACOPO SANNAZARO (199)
33 × 28 in.

TITIAN
Hampton Court

A VENETIAN (207)
41½ × 35 in.

TINTORETTO
Hampton Court

23

TINTORETTO
Hampton Court

THE NINE MUSES (206)
79½ × 120 in.

ESTHER AND AHASUERUS (192)
81 × 105 in.

TINTORETTO
Hampton Court

25

ADORATION OF THE SHEPHERDS (204)
53¾ × 84 in.

JACOPO BASSANO
Hampton Court

26

VERONESE
Hampton Court

THE MARRIAGE OF ST. CATHERINE (194)
58 × 78 in.

27

DOSSO DOSSI   HOLY FAMILY (220)
Hampton Court   66 × 67 in.

SEBASTIANO RICCI   ADORATION OF THE KINGS (265)
Buckingham Palace   130 × 114 in.

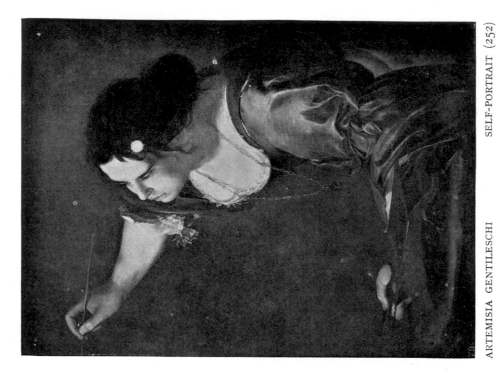

ARTEMISIA GENTILESCHI   SELF-PORTRAIT (252)

Hampton Court   38 × 29 ins.

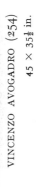

FETI   VINCENZO AVOGADRO (254)

Kensington Palace   45 × 35½ in.

S. RICCI   THE FINDING OF MOSES (414)

Buckingham Palace $27\frac{1}{2} \times 24\frac{1}{2}$ in.

S. RICCI   SACRIFICE OF POLYXENA (418)

Holyrood House 29×25 in.

CANALETTO
Windsor

ST. MARK'S AND THE CAMPANILE (443)
$52\frac{1}{2} \times 67\frac{1}{2}$ in.

LIBRARY AND SALUTE (454)
67 × 52½ in.

CANALETTO
Windsor

THE PIAZZETTA AND S. GIORGIO (441)
67 × 52 in.

CANALETTO
Windsor

CANALETTO   MURANO AND S. MICHELE (437)
Windsor   49 × 52 in.

CANALETTO   SALUTE AND DOGANA (459)
Windsor   18¾ × 31¼ in.

CANALETTO
Windsor

COLLEONI MONUMENT (447)
$36\frac{3}{4} \times 51\frac{1}{2}$ in.

CANALETTO
Windsor

ASCENSION DAY (446)
$30\frac{1}{4} \times 49\frac{1}{2}$ in.

35

CANALETTO
Windsor

ST. PAUL'S (475)
41½ × 73½ in.

36

CANALETTO
Windsor

THE PANTHEON (465)
70¼ × 42 in.

CANALETTO
Windsor

ARCH OF TITUS (457)
74¾ × 41 in.

37

MABUSE

Hampton Court

ADAM AND EVE (144)

65 × 43 in.

MASTER OF THE LUCY LEGEND   MADONNA (173)

Buckingham Palace   16⅜ × 9¾ in.

MEMLING   PORTRAIT (157)
Windsor   12 × 10 in.

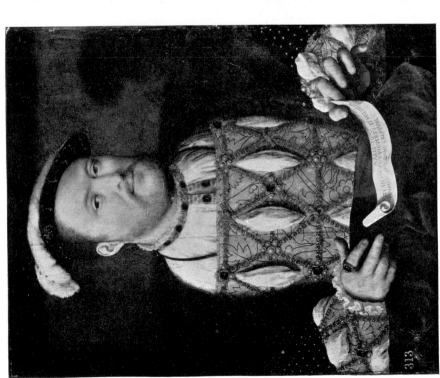

JOOS VAN CLEVE   HENRY VIII (1)
Hampton Court   28 × 22 in.

39

PORTRAIT OF A LADY (283)
32 × 22½ in.

RUBENS
Windsor

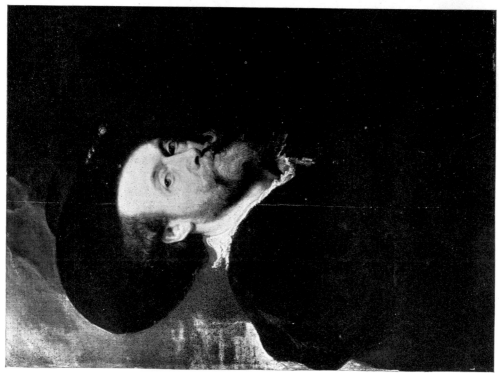

SELF-PORTRAIT (281)
33 × 24 in.

RUBENS
Windsor

40

RUBENS
Windsor

THE GERBIER FAMILY (103)
82¼ × 119 in.

RUBENS
Buckingham Palace

THE ASSUMPTION (279)
$40\frac{1}{4} \times 26$ in.

RUBENS
Windsor

HOLY FAMILY (291)
$84\frac{1}{2} \times 84$ in.

44

RUBENS

ST. GEORGE (288)

Buckingham Palace

60 × 89 in.

45

RUBENS
Buckingham Palace

THE FARM AT LAEKEN (289)
34 × 50 in.

RUBENS   ARCHDUKE ALBERT (287)
Windsor   121 × 85 in.

VAN DYCK   ST. MARTIN (282)
Windsor   94 × 102 in.

DÜRER   A YOUNG MAN (160)
Windsor   12½ × 10 in.

CRANACH   APOLLO AND DIANA (140)
Buckingham Palace   33 × 22¼ in.

HANS HOLBEIN THE YOUNGER
Hampton Court

NOLI ME TANGERE (158)
29½ × 37 in.

49

HANS HOLBEIN THE YOUNGER
Windsor

SIR HENRY GUILDFORD (6)
51¾ × 39¼ in.

50

HANS HOLBEIN THE YOUNGER
Windsor

THE DUKE OF NORFOLK (**10**)
$31\frac{1}{4} \times 21\frac{1}{4}$ in.

51

HANS HOLBEIN THE YOUNGER   WILLIAM RESKIMER (25)

Windsor   17¼ × 12¼ in.

HANS HOLBEIN THE YOUNGER   DERICK BORN (15)

Windsor   23¾ × 17¾ in.

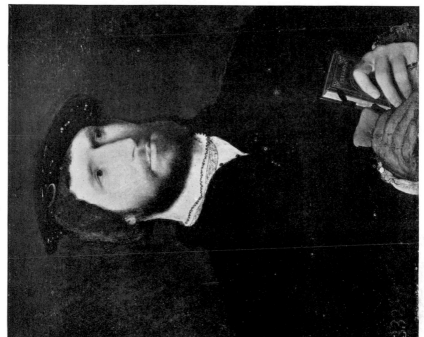

JEAN CLOUET
Windsor

MAN WITH A PETRARCH (156)
$14\frac{3}{4} \times 12\frac{3}{4}$ in.

HANS HOLBEIN THE YOUNGER
Windsor

HANS OF ANTWERP (12)
$24\frac{1}{2} \times 19$ in.

53

EUROPA (416)

40 × 53 in.

CLAUDE LORRAIN

Buckingham Palace

THE YOUNG GAMBLERS (425)
21¼ × 25 in.

MATHIEU LE NAIN
Buckingham Palace

55

GASPAR POUSSIN
Windsor

JONAH AND THE WHALE (396)
38½ × 53 in.

56

PATER   ITALIAN COMEDIANS (410)

Windsor $20\frac{1}{2} \times 25$ in

TER BRUGGHEN   A LAUGHING BRAVO (363)
Hampton Court $4^1 \times 33\frac{1}{2}$ in.

FRANS HALS   A GENTLEMAN (358)
Buckingham Palace $4.5\frac{3}{4} \times 35\frac{1}{2}$ in.

THE SHIPBUILDER AND HIS WIFE (387)
45 × 66¾ in.

REMBRANDT
Buckingham Palace

REMBRANDT   CHRIST AND THE MAGDALEN (333)
Buckingham Palace   24 × 19½ in.

60

REMBRANDT
Buckingham Palace

ADORATION OF THE MAGI (306)
$48\frac{1}{2} \times 40\frac{1}{2}$ in.

61

REMBRANDT   PORTRAIT OF HIS MOTHER (376)
Windsor   23½ × 18 in.

REMBRANDT   LADY WITH A FAN (360)
Buckingham Palace $41\frac{1}{2} \times 33$ in.

VERMEER
Buckingham Palace

A LADY AT THE VIRGINALS (305)
29 × 25¼ in.

TERBORCH   THE LETTER (296)
Buckingham Palace $32\frac{1}{4} \times 26\frac{3}{4}$ in.

65

PIETER DE HOOCH   A COURTYARD IN DELFT (347)
Buckingham Palace $27\frac{1}{4} \times 21\frac{1}{4}$ in.

66

PIETER DE HOOCH
Buckingham Palace

THE CARD PLAYERS (307)
30 × 26 in.

JAN STEEN   THE MORNING TOILET (316)
Buckingham Palace   25½ × 20¾ in.

68

JAN STEEN

Buckingham Palace

TAVERN WITH A FIDDLER (311)
$32\frac{1}{2} \times 27\frac{1}{2}$ in.

69

RUSTICS IN A TAVERN (301)
24¾ × 29¼ in

JAN STEEN
Buckingham Palace

70

METSU   THE 'CELLO PLAYER (326)

Buckingham Palace   24¾ × 18¾ in.

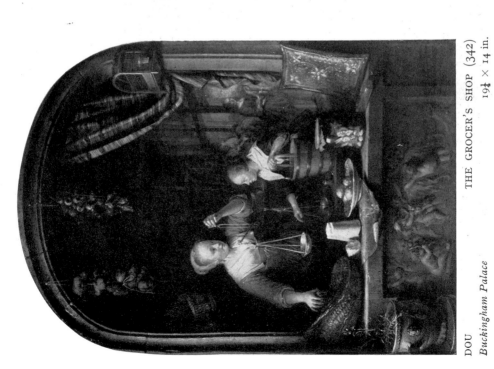

DOU   THE GROCER'S SHOP (342)

Buckingham Palace   19¼ × 14 in.

THE NEGRO PAGE (359)
$56\frac{1}{4} \times 89\frac{1}{4}$ in.

CUYP
Buckingham Palace

72

CUYP

Buckingham Palace

THE PASSAGE BOAT (357)

49 × 56¾ in.

CUYP   GENTLEMAN ON HORSEBACK (329)
Buckingham Palace $27\frac{1}{4} \times 33\frac{3}{4}$ in.

CUYP   THE TROOPER (361)
Buckingham Palace $46 \times 58\frac{1}{2}$ in.

RUISDAEL   THE WINDMILL (371)
Buckingham Palace $29\frac{3}{4} \times 39\frac{3}{4}$ in.

HOBBEMA   THE WATERMILL (302)
Buckingham Palace $21 \times 27\frac{3}{4}$ in.

VAN DER HEYDEN   VIEW OF VEERE (378)
Buckingham Palace   18 × 22 in.

W. VAN DER VELDE   SHIPS IN A CALM (312)
Buckingham Palace   23½ × 28 in.

TENIERS   RUSTICS PLAYING CARDS (352)
Buckingham Palace $9\frac{1}{2} \times 13\frac{1}{2}$ in.

TENIERS   THE DRUMMER (369)
Buckingham Palace $19\frac{1}{2} \times 25\frac{3}{4}$ in.

TENIERS
Buckingham Palace

A VILLAGE FESTIVAL (372)
33¾ × 43½ in.

78

VILLAGERS DANCING (365)
$32\frac{1}{2} \times 49\frac{3}{4}$ in.

TENIERS
Buckingham Palace

79

ADRIAEN VAN OSTADE   A PEASANT'S COTTAGE (325)

Buckingham Palace   19½ × 16¼ in.

SCHALCKEN   A FAMILY CONCERT (336)

Buckingham Palace   22¾ × 18¾ in.

THE HERDSMAN (370)
$12\frac{1}{4} \times 15\frac{1}{4}$ in.

DU JARDIN
Buckingham Palace

UNKNOWN ARTIST   PRINCESS ELIZABETH (24)

Windsor   42¾ × 32¼ in.

GHEERAERTS (?)   HENRY, PRINCE OF WALES, AND LORD ESSEX (5)

Hampton Court   75 × 65 in.

GHEERAERTS (?) LADY·ARABELLA STUART (11) 85½ × 53½ in.
Hampton Court

VAN SOMER QUEEN ANNE OF DENMARK (19) 103 × 82 in.
Windsor

WILLIAM OF ORANGE (18)
85 × 49 in.

HONTHORST
Windsor

CHARLES I (20)
80¼ × 51 in.

MYTENS
Windsor

84

VAN DYCK
Windsor

THREE CHILDREN OF CHARLES I (34)
53 × 60 ins.

VAN DYCK   QUEEN HENRIETTA MARIA (37)
Windsor   28¼ × 22¼ in.

VAN DYCK   KING CHARLES I (30)
Windsor   33¼ × 39¼ in.

VAN DYCK   THE DUCHESS OF RICHMOND (39)
Windsor $73\frac{3}{4} \times 54\frac{1}{2}$ in.

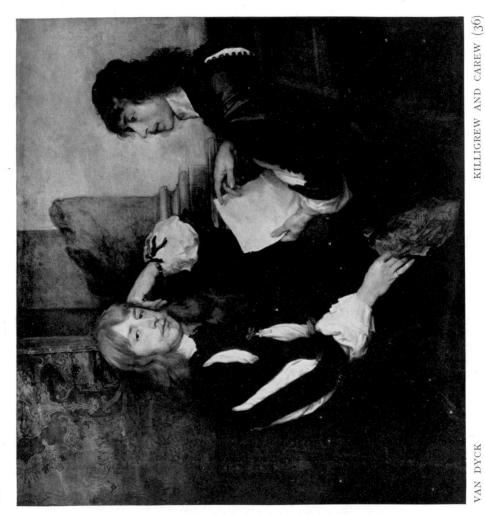

VAN DYCK
Windsor

KILLIGREW AND CAREW (36)
$52\frac{1}{4} \times 56\frac{1}{2}$ in.

SELF-PORTRAIT (43)
27 × 23 in.

MYTENS
Hampton Court

JAMES II (29)
37½ × 31¼ in.

DOBSON
Windsor

LELY   LADY BYRON (99)
Hampton Court   63 × 50¼ in.

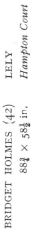

RILEY   BRIDGET HOLMES (42)
Windsor   88¾ × 58½ in.

KNELLER   A CHINESE CONVERT (116) $83\frac{1}{2} \times 58$ in.
Kensington Palace

HUYSMANS   QUEEN CATHERINE OF BRAGANZA (117) $85\frac{1}{2} \times 58\frac{1}{2}$ in.
Windsor

RAMSAY   QUEEN CHARLOTTE (95) $97\frac{3}{4} \times 63\frac{1}{2}$ in.
Buckingham Palace

REYNOLDS   GRAF SCHAUMBURG-LIPPE (108) $95\frac{1}{2} \times 80\frac{1}{2}$ in.
St. James's Palace

REYNOLDS   THE DUKE OF YORK (115)

Buckingham Palace   93½ × 56½ in.

REYNOLDS   LORD RODNEY (100)

St. James's Palace   93 × 57 in.

GARRICK AS KITELY (92)
30¼ × 25 in.

REYNOLDS
Windsor

SELF-PORTRAIT (89)
30 × 25 in.

REYNOLDS
Windsor

94

GAINSBOROUGH　　　　　　　　　　THE DUKE AND DUCHESS OF CUMBERLAND (82)
Windsor　　　　　　　　　　　　　　　　　　　　　　　$64\frac{1}{2} \times 49$ in.

97

GAINSBOROUGH
Buckingham Palace

COL. ST. LEGER (112)
$97\frac{1}{2} \times 73\frac{3}{4}$ in.

98

GAINSBOROUGH
Buckingham Palace

JOHANN CHRISTIAN FISCHER (110)
$89\frac{1}{2} \times 58\frac{3}{4}$ in.

GAINSBOROUGH

Buckingham Palace

DIANA AND ACTAEON (478)

61 × 73 in.

ZOFFANY
Windsor

QUEEN CHARLOTTE AND HER FAMILY (65)
$41\frac{1}{2} \times 50$ in.

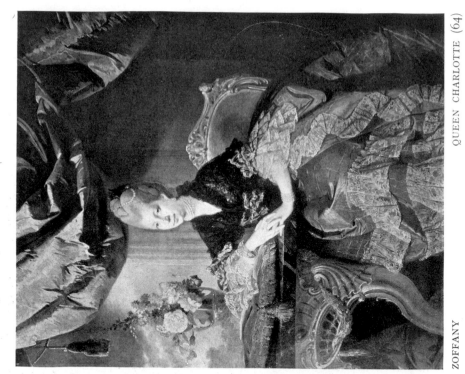

QUEEN CHARLOTTE (64)
65 × 53 in.

ZOFFANY
Windsor

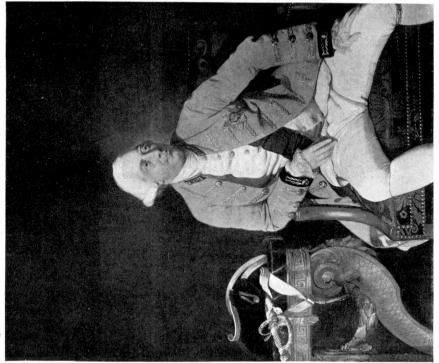

KING GEORGE III (62)
64 × 52½ in.

ZOFFANY
Windsor

102

THE TRIBUNA (48)
47½ × 59½ in.

ZOFFANY
Windsor

ZOFFANY
Windsor

QUEEN CHARLOTTE IN HER DRESSING ROOM (63)
$44\frac{1}{4} \times 50$ in.

104

SYDNEY MEDOWS (481)
$32\frac{3}{4} \times 40$ in.

STUBBS
Windsor

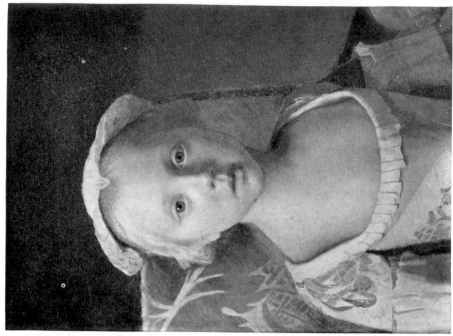

PRINCESS LOUISA ANNE (74g)
17¼ × 14 in.

LIOTARD
Windsor

PRINCESS SOPHIA (57)
29¾ × 23¾ in.

HOPPNER
Windsor

106

DUC DE RICHELIEU (125)
51 × 42 in.

LAWRENCE
Windsor

SIR WILLIAM CURTIS (118)
35½ × 28 in.

LAWRENCE
Windsor

107

LAWRENCE   POPE PIUS VII (131)
Windsor   105 × 68 in.

LAWRENCE
Windsor

ARCHDUKE CHARLES (127)
105 × 68¾ in.

109

WILKIE   THE PENNY WEDDING (499)
Buckingham Palace $25\frac{1}{2} \times 37\frac{1}{2}$ in.

WILKIE   A SPANISH POSADA (483)
Buckingham Palace $29\frac{1}{2} \times 36$ in.

WINTERHALTER   THE FIRST OF MAY (56)
Windsor   42 × 51 in.

WILKIE   QUEEN VICTORIA'S FIRST COUNCIL (51)
Windsor $60\frac{3}{4} \times 94\frac{3}{4}$ in.

INDEX

NOTE.—*The first figures refer to the pages of this Souvenir and those in brackets to the number of the work in the Exhibition.*

LONDON: MADE AND PRINTED IN GREAT BRITAIN BY WILLIAM CLOWES AND SONS, LTD.